Play-Ground Theatre

Celebrating 20 years!

THEATRE GAMES FOR ELEMENTARY SCHOOL CHILDREN AGES 7-12

Creative dramatic exercises to enhance the classroom, after school, birthday parties, or summer camps

Theatre Games for Elementary School Children Ages 7-12
Copyright ©2009 by Play-Ground Theatre Company, Inc.

FIRST EDITION
Printed in the United States of America

Published by:
Play-Ground Theatre Company, Inc.
169 Albert Drive, P.O. Box 58 Rollinsville, CO 80474
http://www.playgroundtheatre.com

THEATRE GAMES FOR ELEMENTARY SCHOOL CHILDREN AGES 7-12

FIRST EDITION

By Mia Sole & Jeff Haycock

Table of Contents

Table of Contents

Table of Contents

*"Do not train children to learning by force and harshness,
but direct them to it by what amuses their minds, so that you may
be better able to discover with accuracy the genius of each."*
- Plato -

📖 How to use this book

This book is divided into two parts:

Part One

- ☺ **Circle Games**
- ☼ **Warm-up**
- ↔ **Crossing Games**
- ★ **Acting Games**

Each section includes fifteen theatre games that you can play with your students. Every creative dramatic exercise offers teachers easy-to-follow directions:

How to play
Step-by-step instructions to guide you through each game

Objective
The goal of each game

Notes
Additional information

Materials
Supplies needed for the game 👤

Part Two

🎭 **Create Characters, Scenes, Scripts & Songs**

This section includes fifteen characters designed for creative exploration. Each character offers worksheets for you to copy and hand out.

Students invent their own characters, create lines, and develop scenes that lead to scripting, song writing, and original works of art. With these worksheets, you can inspire your student's individual creativity, and make learning fun!

Play-Ground Theatre

Part One

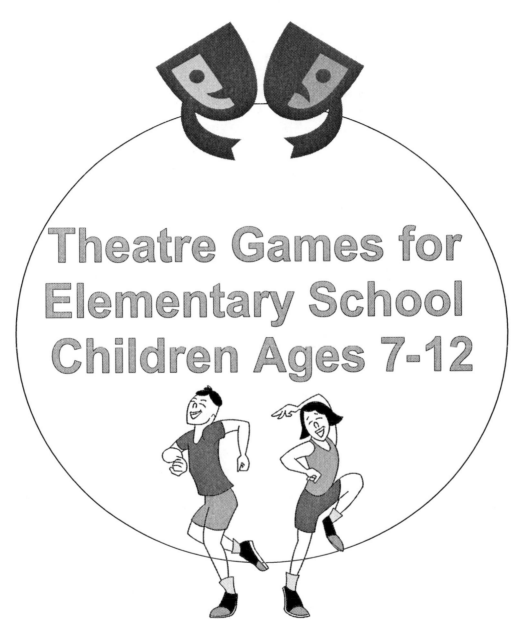

Theatre Games for
Elementary School
Children Ages 7-12

Circle Games, Warm-up
Crossing & Acting Games

Play-Ground Theatre Circle Games

This section provides teachers with Circle Games designed to stimulate, motivate, and energize elementary school children.

Play-Ground Theatre's Circle Games allow students the chance to explore their creativity, learn to communicate, develop better listening skills, and practice patience in a group setting. As you continue to play these games, you will notice improvements in students' attention spans.

Circle Games set a positive, engaging, and upbeat mood. So round up your students, and share in the joy of creative dramatics.

Circle Games Included:

Follow the Leader

We're Great!

What's on your Mind?

Pass the Object

Emotion Circle

What are you Doing?

Play in a Paper Bag

Favorite/Least Favorite

Zapp!

Character Circle

Meeting of the Minds

Share

Energy Circle

Imaginary Places

Positive Cheer

Circle Game ☺ Instructions

❶ Start with students sitting in a circle.

❷ Teacher announces the Circle Game.

❸ Teacher gives students instructions.

❹ Students have a chance to express themselves, and participate with the class.

☺ Follow the Leader

How to play

❶ Start with students sitting in a circle.

❷ Tell the students that they're going to copy your movements.

❸ Begin by performing movements using the suggestions below such as flexing muscles.

❹ Have the class copy as many movements as you wish.

❺ Then call on students, one at a time, to lead the class.

Note: If students have trouble leading, provide suggestions or allow them to pass.

❻ After a few moments, ask the next student to lead the class.

❼ When everyone has had a turn, the game is complete.

Follow the Leader Suggestions

clapping hands	shrugging shoulders	snapping fingers
patting the knees	yawning	lifting one leg
touching toes	patting your head	wiggling fingers
nodding head	pointing your finger	leaning side to side

Objective: Focus on listening skills, concentration, and following instructions.

 We're Great!

How to play

❶Start with students sitting in a circle.

❷Ask students to place their hands in the center of the circle.

❸Have the students lift up their hands and say, "Weeeeeeeeeeeeeeeeeee're Great!"

❹Ask students to place their hands in the center of the circle again.

❺This time have the students lift up their hands and say, "Weeeeeeeeeeeeeeeeee're smart!"

❻Ask students to place their hands in the center again.

❼Have the students lift up their hands and say, "Weeeeeeeeeeeeeeeeee're healthy!"

❽Ask students to place their hands in the center again.

❾Have the students lift up their hands and say, "Weeeeeeeeeeeeeeeeee're incredibly attractive!"

❿Finally, ask students to place their hands in the center again, lift up their hands and say, "Weeeeeeeeeeeeeeeeeee're Great!"

Note: You may also add the name of your school, mascot, club, camp, family, classroom, etc. such as "Weeeeeeee're Cougars!"

Objective: Build self-esteem, confidence, team skills, and create unity in the class.

☺ What's on your Mind?

How to play

❶ Start with students sitting in a circle.

❷ Ask students to share something they have been thinking about.

❸ Go around the circle and have the class say,

"What's on your mind _____?"

Fill student's name in the blank.

❹ Each student, one at a time, shares what's on his/her mind.

❺ When everyone has had a turn, the game is complete.

Note: If a student would not like a turn, they may pass. Encourage answers to be concise, however, if a student has an important issue to discuss, take extra time to listen. Remind students to be polite, quiet, and not to interrupt each other.

Objective: Provide a sharing and safe environment for students to discuss their thoughts.

☺ Pass the Object

How to play

❶ Start with students sitting in a circle.

❷ Tell students to pretend they have an invisible object in their hands.

❸ Instruct the class to imagine that the object can be heavy or light, soft or hard, big or small.

Note: You may want to demonstrate creating a make-believe object for students to understand the pantomime concept. For example: pretend to blow up a large balloon or struggle to pick up a heavy rock.

❹ After students have made their make-believe objects, have everyone toss them into the middle of the circle.

❺ The teacher reaches in and pretends to make one big object.

❻ Pretend it's heavy. Then pass it to the first student, who molds it into a new shape, and passes it to the next student in the circle.

❼ The student takes it, changes the object, passes it to the next student, and so on.

❽ When everyone has had a turn, the teacher makes the object smaller and smaller, until it disappears into the air.

Objective: Activate imaginations by introducing the art of pantomime.

☺ Emotion Circle

<u>How to play</u>

❶Start with students sitting in a circle.

❷Tell the class that they're going to act out different emotions.

❸Select an emotion using the suggestions below such as happy.

❹Demonstrate happy by smiling and giggling. Then ask students to act happy with you, smiling and giggling.

❺Change the emotion to sad. Demonstrate sad by frowning and crying.

❻Ask students to act sad with you, frowning and crying.

❼Choose three or more emotions for the class to perform using the suggestions below.

<u>Emotion Circle Suggestions</u>

excited	peaceful	cool	shy
terrified	happy	indifferent	tired
sick	angry	relaxed	surprised
nervous	exhausted	sneaky	sad
nosy	stubborn	wild	bossy

Objective: Learn how we process different emotions.

☺ What are you Doing?

How to play

❶ Start with students standing in a circle.

❷ Begin the game by stepping in the middle of the circle, and performing an action such as fly-fishing.

❸ The class says, "What are you doing?"

❹ The teacher responds, "I'm fly-fishing. Everybody try!"

❺ The class performs the action (fishing) together.

❻ Then the teacher steps out of the circle. The first student steps in, and performs a new action such as brushing your teeth.

❼ The class says, "What are you doing?"

❽ Student says, "I'm brushing my teeth. Everybody try!"

❾ The class performs the action (brushing teeth) together.

❿ The student steps out of the circle. The next student steps in and begins a new action. Repeat until everyone has had a turn.

Note: If a student has trouble performing in the circle, provide suggestions or allow them to pass.

Objective: Improve individual performance skills and develop creative thinking.

☺ Play in a Paper Bag

Materials

one paper bag per student
three props for each bag

How to play

❶ Collect one paper bag with three props inside for each student playing the game.

❷ Start with students sitting in a circle.

❸ Tell students that they're going to make up a short play using props from a paper bag.

❹ Give each student a paper bag with three props inside, and allow them time to prepare their plays.

❺ Ask students to raise their hands when they're ready for a turn.

❻ Select students, one at a time, to perform.

❼ When everyone has had a turn, the game is complete.

Note: Props can be any items you find in your classroom or around the house. For example: toys, stuffed animals, books, craft materials, photographs, etc.

Objective: Stimulate individual creativity and self-expression through story telling.

☺ Favorite/Least Favorite

How to play

❶ Start with students sitting in a circle.

❷ Tell students they're going to share their favorite, and least favorite things.

❸ Choose a topic using the suggestions below such as foods.

❹ Select students, one at a time, to share their favorites.

❺ After all students have had a turn, ask them to share their least favorites.

❻ Choose three or more topics or make up your own.

Note: You may ask students to suggest additional topics.

Favorite/Least Favorite Suggestions

clothes	pizza toppings	movies
seasons	hobbies	games
sports teams	music groups	vacations
songs	teachers	books

Objective: Acknowledge each student's feelings and share common interests.

☺ Zapp!

How to play

❶ Start with students sitting in a circle.

❷ Follow this dialog with the class:

Teacher: "It's time to play Zapp! Everyone say Zapp!"

Students: "Zapp!"

Teacher: "Okay, everyone reach up and put your hands on your head, and pull anything negative out.
For example, if you have a cold or feel tired,
pull out that bad stuff and place it in front of you."

Spend a moment pulling out bad stuff with students.

Teacher: "Now we're going to take all this bad stuff and 'Zapp!' it into good stuff. Everyone lift up your arms, wiggle your fingers and say… Ooooooooooh Zapp!"

Students: "Ooooooooooh Zapp!"

Teacher: "Okay, let's try it together."

Class lifts up their arms, wiggles their fingers and says, "Zapp!"

Students: "Ooooooooooh ZAPP!"

Teacher: "One more time."

Students: "Ooooooooooh ZAPP!"

Teacher: "Last time with a little more energy!"

Students: "Ooooooooooh ZAPP!"

Teacher: "Great! Now reach down in front of you.
              Scoop up all the good stuff, put it back into your head.
              Sit up straight, brush your hair, fix your clothes and say,
              I feel great!"

Students: "I feel great!"

Teacher: "Everyone say, I'm having a great day!"

Students: "I'm having a great day!"

Teacher: "Excellent job!"

Objective: Focus on removing negativity, replacing it with positive energy.

☺ Character Circle

How to play

❶ Start with students sitting in a circle.

❷ Ask students to think of their favorite character.

❸ Tell students that they're going to introduce themselves pretending to be their favorite characters.

❹ Have students raise their hands when their ready for a turn.

❺ Select a student to say their character name, and share something they like to do as that character.

❻ When each student is finished, the class says, "Nice to meet you _____!" *Insert character name in the blank.*

❼ When everyone has had a turn, the game is complete.

Note: If a student has trouble thinking of a character, they may pass, use their real name, or choose from suggestions below.

Character Circle Suggestions

superheroes	scientists	rock stars	detectives
cowboys	princesses	villains	knights
fairies	magicians	billionaires	ghosts

Objective: Increase self-confidence and dramatic skills by acting as different characters.

☺ Meeting of the Minds

How to play

❶ Start with students sitting in a circle.

❷ Tell students that they're going to play a game called Meeting of the Minds, during which they're all going to be geniuses.

❸ Select a topic for discussion using the suggestions below, and announce it to the class. Then introduce the first speaker.

❹ Each student takes a turn pretending to be an expert on that topic.

❺ When the discussion is complete, choose another topic.

❻ Select three or more topics for discussion.

Note: Students may suggest additional topics, develop genius names, or character traits to enhance each discussion.

Meeting of the Minds Suggestions

eating rituals of boa constrictors

bird calls of the Amazon

hair styles of early cave dwellers

hot fudge sundae making

mammals of Tasmania

famous works of clown poets

night blooming plants on Mars

advantages of electric cars

pizza eating techniques

clothing styles in China

musical instruments of the arctic

dance moves of the dung beetle

Objective: Boost self-assurance and align the mind to super intelligence.

☺ **Share**

<u>Materials</u>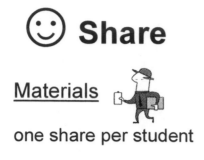

one share per student

<u>How to play</u>

Note: First tell students to bring something from home they would like to share. For example: a book, toy, photograph, or drawing.

❶Ask students to get their shares and sit in a circle.

❷Everyone says, "Share, share, it's time for share."

❸Call on students, one at a time, to share their item and talk a little bit about it.

❹Ask the class to thank the student for sharing.

❺Select the next student who is ready for a turn.

❻When everyone has shared with the class, the game is complete.

Note: If a student doesn't bring a share, they can tell a story, a joke, or pass. As an alternative, teachers may ask students to find their favorite toy in the classroom, and bring it to the circle for share.

Objective: Develop verbal, interactive, and listening skills through sharing.

☺ Energy Circle

How to play

❶Start with students sitting in a circle.

❷Tell students that they're going to send energy around the circle, by gently squeezing hands.

❸Ask students to join hands.

❹Tell students that when they feel one hand squeezed, they pass it to the next student, by gently squeezing their other hand.

❺Start the game by squeezing the hand of the student to your left.

❻Allow students to pass energy around the circle until everyone has had a turn.

❼Teacher starts again and reverses the direction.

❽Pass the energy around the circle three or more times.

Note: Students may speed up, slow down, or reverse the energy in the circle. You may also want to play this game to unify a cast before beginning a performance.

Objective: Connect students by sending energy around the circle.

☺ Imaginary Places

How to play

❶Start with students sitting in a circle.

❷Tell students that they're going to make up a short story about an imaginary place. This special place can be wherever each student wants.

❸Ask students to raise their hands when they're ready for a turn.

❹Select a student to describe their imaginary place. Then each student asks a question about the story. For example:

- Where is this place?

- Who lives there?

- What can you do there for fun?

- How long does it take to get there?

- What language do they speak?

❺Students take turns telling stories and answering questions about their imaginary places.

❻When everyone has had a turn creating a place, the game is complete.

Note: Encourage students to add as much detail to their locations as possible. If a student has trouble making up an imaginary place, they may pass.

Objective: Fuse language and imagination to create make-believe lands.

☺ Positive Cheer

How to play

❶ Start with students sitting in a circle.

❷ Tell students the importance of teamwork and keeping a positive attitude.

❸ Ask students to join you in a positive class cheer.

❹ Have students make a drum roll, tapping their legs to make the sound.

❺ Teacher goes around the circle and says,

"Let's hear it for _____ !"

Fill in the blank with each student's name.

❻ The student stands up, takes a bow, and the class applauds.

Note: When delivering each student's name, use a nice loud stage voice, and have fun with the class.

❼ When everyone has been cheered for, the game is complete.

Objective: Build self-esteem and confidence in a positive atmosphere.

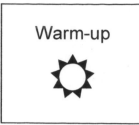

Warm-up

Play-Ground Theatre Warm-up

Warm-up is focused on limbering up the body, voice, and mind. Get ready to lead invigorating warm-up exercises that increase concentration and create magical environments children love.

Vocal Warm-up exercises are specially devised for students to use their imaginations, by making the sounds of animals, objects, locations, and characters.

Physical Warm-up helps the class develop coordination, rhythm, and motor skills. Jumping, stretching, and physical fitness energizes the class.

Warm-ups Included:

Stand-up, Sit-down	Story Around the Circle
Tongue Twister	The Exerciser
Heads in, Feet out	Shakespearean Circle
Shake! Shake! Shake!	Character Voices
Yes/No Circle	Zing!
Acting the Alphabet	Mirror Game
The Conductor	Statue Garden
If You're Ready	

Warm-up ✪ Instructions

❶ Start with students in a circle.

❷ Teacher announces the Warm-up activity.

❸ Teacher gives students instructions.

❹ Students have a chance to warm-up vocally and physically.

☼ Stand-up, Sit-down

How to play

❶ Start with students sitting in a circle.

❷ Teacher says, "Okay everybody, it's time to warm-up. So, let's all stand up!" Teacher and students stand up.

❸ Teacher says, "Great job everyone! But, wait a minute, I think we're supposed to sit down." Teacher and students sit down.

❹ Teacher says, "Hold on a second (teacher pauses and thinks), we start standing up." All students stand up.

❺ Teacher says, "No, it was sitting." All students sit down again.

❻ Teacher continues to change his/her mind while the class stands up and sits down, over and over again.

❼ To end the game students say, "This is getting ridiculous!"

Objective: Create a joyous, comfortable atmosphere that's fun and silly.

☀ Story Around the Circle

How to play

❶ Start with students sitting in a circle.

❷ Tell the class that they're going to make up a story where each student adds one or two sentences, passing the story around the circle.

❸ Choose and announce the theme for the fist story using the suggestions below.

❹ Begin the story by saying, "Once upon a time there was_____ ."
Fill in the blank with the story theme.

❺ Each student adds one or two sentences to the story.

❻ End the story by saying, "And that is the story of _____ ."
Fill in the blank with the story theme.

Note: Encourage students to invent interesting characters, story lines, voices, or songs that complement the theme.

Story Around the Circle Suggestions

a stinky skunk	a one room school	a bowl of pasta
a monkey from mars	an ugly toad	a beautiful rose garden
a wishing well	a big busy city	a mean bully
a soccer game	a pumpkin patch	a very old grandma

Objective: Increase creative development and teamwork by telling short stories around the circle.

☀ Tongue Twisters

How to play

❶ Start with students standing in a circle.

❷ Tell the class to repeat each line after you, matching your voice, tone, and inflection.

❸ Repeat three or more Tongue Twisters using the suggestion below.

❹ Ask students to think of a Tongue Twister for the class to repeat.

❺ Ask students to raise their hands when they're ready to deliver their line.

❻ Select a student to say his/her line, and the class repeats.

❼ When everyone has had a turn, the game is complete.

Tongue Twisters Suggestions

- Seven slick, slimy snakes slowly, sliding southward.
- Four furious friends fought for the phone.
- She sells seashells by the seashore.
- A quick, witted cricket critic.
- I scream, you scream, we all scream for ice cream.
- Chester Cheetah chews a chunk of cheap cheddar cheese.
- The thirty three thieves thought that they thrilled the throne throughout Thursday.

Objective: To sharpen pronunciation as you limber up the lips and tongue.

 # The Exerciser

How to play

❶Start with students standing in a circle.

❷Ask students to take one giant step back and spread out so they have plenty of room.

❸Tell students that each one will have a chance to lead the class as "The Exerciser."

❹Introduce yourself to the class as "The Exerciser" by flexing big muscles and saying, "I am the Exerciser!"

Note: When you introduce yourself as "The Exerciser" you may want to imitate the voice of Arnold Schwarzenegger.

❺Ask the class to follow your physical movements as you lead the first exercise such as touching your toes.

❻Begin the exercise by asking the class to say, "Let's do it!"

❼Perform the exercise together for a few moments.

❽Ask students to raise their hands for a turn to become "The Exerciser" and lead the class.

❾When everyone has had a turn, the game is complete.

Objective: Engage the class in physical movements designed to make the body stronger.

☀ Heads in, Feet out

How to play

❶Start by asking students to lie on their backs in a circle with their heads in the center, and their feet facing out.

❷Tell the class that they're going to make different sounds together. When the teacher raises his/her hands, the sound will be louder. When the teacher lowers his/her hands, the sound will be softer.

❸Ask the class to begin by softly humming. Teacher raises his/her hands to make the sound louder, and then lowers them to make the sound soft again.

❹Ask the class to start laughing. Teacher raises his/her hands to make the sound louder, and then lowers them to make the sound softer.

❺Ask the class to make the sounds of birds singing, use your hands again to adjust the volume.

❻Select three or more sounds using the suggestions below or ask the class to suggest things they would like to hear.

Heads in, Feet out Suggestions

wind blowing	stadium cheering	pinball machine
thunder	grocery store	grandfather clock
drumming	chorus singing	computers
raindrops	jungle animals	popcorn popping

Objective: Creating sounds together at different volumes.

☼ Shakespearean Circle

How to play

❶ Start with students standing up.

❷ Tell students that they're going to deliver lines from famous Shakespearean characters.

❸ Begin by asking students to raise their hands if they are familiar with William Shakespeare or his plays.

Note: Ask students to share their knowledge of Shakespeare's plays or any productions they have seen.

❹ Select three or more lines to repeat with the class using the suggestions below.

Shakespearean Circle Suggestions

"To be, or not to be: that is the question." **Hamlet - Act III, Scene I**

"Friends, Romans, countrymen, lend me your ears; I come to bury Caesar, not to praise him." **Julius Caesar - Act III, Scene II**

"Double, double toil and trouble; Fire burn, and cauldron bubble." **Macbeth - Act IV, Scene I**

"O Romeo, Romeo! wherefore art thou Romeo?" **Romeo and Juliet - Act II, Scene II**

"All the world 's a stage, and all the men and women merely players. They have their exits and their entrances; And one man in his time plays many parts." **As You Like It - Act II, Scene VII**

Objective: Encourage knowledge and curiosity about the works of William Shakespeare.

☀ Shake! Shake! Shake!

How to play

❶ Have the students to form a standing circle.

❷ Ask the class to shake out their legs.

❸ Ask the class to shake out their feet.

❹ Ask the class to shake out their arms.

❺ Ask the class to shake out their hands.

❻ To end the warm up, ask the class to shake out their whole body.

Note: You can add comedy by asking students to shake out other parts of their bodies. For example: hair, noses, ears, fingernails, spleens, livers, or eyelids.

Objective: Work out the body and make exercise fun.

☼ Character Voices

How to play

❶ Start with students standing up.

❷ Tell the class they're going to repeat lines using character voices.

❸ Select three or more lines to repeat with the class using the suggestions below.

❹ Ask students to raise their hands if they want to suggest a character voice and line for the class to repeat.

Note: Feel free to create new character voices or lines.

❺ When everyone has had a turn to lead, the game is complete.

Character	Line
Inventor	"The experiment is a success! I'm a genius."
Knight	"Hark, who goes there!"
Cowboy/girl	"Howdy partners! Let's ride, rope, and wrangle."
Robot	"Hello, I am a robot."
Caveman	Unga bunga bunga!"
Baby	"Goo goo ga ga goo goo. I want my bottle!"
Skydiver	"Ready, one two, three juuuuummmmmmp."

Objective: Encourage vocal expression and develop character-acting skills.

☀ Yes/No Circle

How to play

❶ Start with students standing in a circle.

❷ Tell students that they will alternate saying, "Yes" or "No" around the circle.

❸ Begin the game by saying, "Yes!" to the student on your right,

❹ The student on your right says, "No!" passing it on to the next student.

❺ The next student says, "Yes!" and so on around the circle.

❻ Continue to the right, alternating "Yes" and "No" until everyone has had a turn. Switch directions and begin again. If you have an even number of students, you may want to start again by saying, "No!" This way students will have a chance to deliver both words.

❼ When everyone has had a turn to say both words, the game is complete.

Note: After playing this game, you may want to discuss how tone of voice and inflection affect the way you communicate.

Objective: Increase understanding of verbal communication using tone of voice and inflection.

☼ Zing!

How to play

❶ Start with students standing up.

❷ Tell students to lift their arms and magically wiggle their fingers.

❸ Explain that they will shoot magic from their fingertips towards the teacher and say, "Zing!"

❹ Teacher counts to three and the students "Zing!" their magical energy.

❺ The teacher reacts by jumping back, acting surprised at the magical powers of the class.

Note: For this exercise, the most important thing is to play up the magical power of the class. With each "Zing!" react as if the classes power is pushing you back further and further.

❻ Ask the class to "Zing!" you three or more times, building their intensity.

❼ Compliment students on their magical abilities.

Objective: Empower the class, acknowledging their energy and magical abilities.

☀ Acting the Alphabet

How to play

❶ Start with students standing in a circle.

❷ Tell students that they're going to take turns suggesting words that begin with each letter of the alphabet. One student will say a word, and the class acts out the word together.

❸ Begin the game by saying a word the starts with the letter "A" such as alligator.

❹ Students perform the suggested word for the letter "A" together.

Note: For continued learning, ask students to spell the words before performing.

❺ The next student in the circle suggests a word that begins with the letter "B" such as bats.

❻ Students perform the suggested word for the letter "B" together.

❼ Continue around the circle until you have performed the entire alphabet.

Note: As students increase their skills, try this game with a timer, and see how fast your class can go.

Objective: Learn the alphabet through performance.

 # Mirror Game

How to play

❶ Start with students standing up.

❷ Ask students to copy your movements as if they're looking in a mirror.

❸ Demonstrate an action slowly, like stretching your arms above your head, then lowering them down to your sides.

❹ Ask students to follow and mirror the action.

❺ Lead the class with three or more actions using the suggestions below. Then select students who would like a turn to lead the group.

❻ The class mirrors each student.

❼ When everyone has had a turn, the game is complete.

Mirror Game Suggestions

putting on boots	blowing up a balloon	picking apples
on a balance beam	eating a banana	on one foot
waving hello	washing hands	meditating
knitting a scarf	taking a bath	painting a wall
braiding hair	face painting	flossing teeth

Objective: Improve concentration and promote working together.

☀ The Conductor

How to play

❶Ask students to form a standing circle.

❷Tell students that they're going to warm-up their voices by singing. Teacher uses hand gestures like a conductor to direct the sound.

❸First teach students the hand gestures using the suggestions below.

❹Begin by taking a deep breath and singing, "Laaaaaaaaahhhh," then ask the class to join in.

❺Ask students to match your notes and follow along as you conduct.

Note: Encourage the class to breathe together between each gesture. You may also try switching singing gestures really fast.

❻Sing three or more notes and conduct the class.

Conductor Hand Gestures	Meaning
raising both hands up	sing louder
lowering both hands down	sing softer
wiggling fingers up	sing higher
wiggling fingers down	sing lower
clasp hands	stop singing
unclasp hands	start singing

Objective: Guide the class to feel confident and playful with their singing voices.

☀ Statue Garden

How to play

❶ Start with students standing up together as if they're on stage.

❷ Tell students that they're going to pretend to be statues in a statue garden.

❸ Announce the title of the Statue Garden using the suggestions below. Then ask students to turn around.

❹ On the count of three, the class turns back around, facing the audience while striking a statue pose.

❺ Clap for students and announce another Statue Garden title.

❻ Give the class three or more titles to perform using the suggestions below or make up your own.

Statue Garden Suggestions

superstars	lost in the woods	mythological beasts
deep in the ocean	the Halloween brew	the surprise party
the square dance	the fire drill	blind mice
zero gravity	the rollercoaster	milking the cow
stinky socks	rock & roll	the tea party
the bad day	the beach party	puppy power

> *Objective: Coach the class in quick, creative thinking while using pantomime.*

☀ If You're Ready

<u>How to play</u>

❶ Start with students standing up.

❷ Tell students to listen to instructions and follow your movements.

❸ Teacher repeats the following lines with a loud voice, rhythmically while performing the motions.

"If you're ready put your hands on your head!
Teacher and students put hands on head.

If you're ready put your hands on your nose!
Teacher and students put hands on nose.

If you're ready put your hands on your knees!
Teacher and students put hands on knees.

If you're ready put your hands on your toes. Knees! Toes!
Teacher and students put hands on toes, then knees and toes.

Knees! Toes! If you're ready say… I'm READY!"
Teacher and students put hands on knees and toes.

❹ Students mirror the actions and say, "I'm READY!"

Note: This warm-up is a great way to focus students at any time, or as a transition from one activity to another. You may also want to vary the commands. For example: "If you're ready put your hands on your hips, elbows, shoulders, hair, or ankles."

Objective: Focus the student's attention, uniting the class with an upbeat, positive attitude.

Crossing
Games

Play-Ground Theatre Crossing Games

Play-Ground Theatre Crossing Games connect students by allowing everyone to pretend and participate together. They offer students a chance to cross the space, exploring different emotions, people, animals, or characters. This fuses physical and artistic expression with creative movement.

Students are instructed to raise their hands if they would like a turn. The student receives instructions and leads the group or suggests an idea and crosses the space while the class follows. When the class has crossed the space, the teacher selects another student.
If a student would not like a turn, they may pass.

Crossing Games Included:

Sports Stars

Body Moving

Changing Environments

Stages of Life

Copy Cat

Emergencies

Action/Reaction

Character Crossing

Take a Walk

Without Words

Emotion Crossing

Working with Animals

Greeting Game

Add-on

Slow Motion

Crossing Game ⟷ Instructions

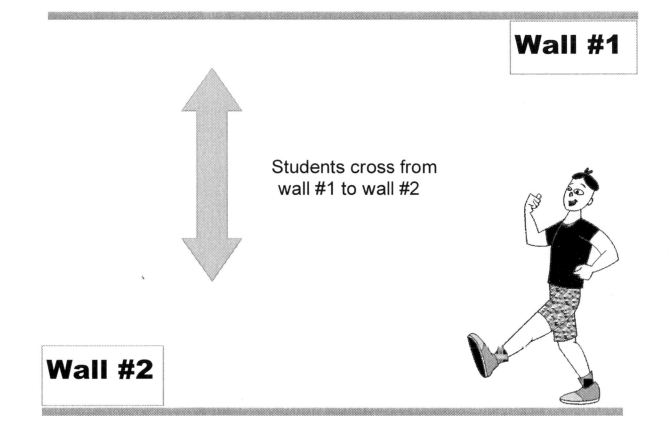

Wall #1

Students cross from wall #1 to wall #2

Wall #2

❶ Start with students lined up, ready to act.

❷ Teacher gives instructions for the Crossing Game.

❸ Students take turns leading the group.

❹ Students cross the space acting.

❺ Students line up for the next turn.

←→Sports Stars

How to play

❶ Start with students lined up, ready to act across the room.

❷ Ask students to think of their favorite sport.

❸ Students raise their hands when they are ready for a turn.

❹ Select a student to announce his/her sport.

❺ Students cross the room pretending to play that sport.

❻ At the end of each turn, ask one or two students to demonstrate the sport in front of the class.

❼ Select another student to suggest a different sport, and cross playing.

❽ When everyone has had a turn, the game is complete.

Sports Stars Suggestions

basketball	volleyball	football	water polo
fencing	water skiing	ice skating	snow boarding
skiing	hockey	baseball	kick ball
soccer	tennis	bowling	karate

Objective: Assimilate athletic skills with creative dramatic play.

←→Take a Walk

❶Start with students lined up, ready to act across the space.

❷Tell students they're going to take a walk through different things.

❸Ask students to cross the space using the suggestions below such as walking through spider webs.

❹Class crosses the space performing the suggestion, for this example, walking through spider webs.

❺Between each turn, ask students to line up, listening for the next instruction.

❻Choose three or more things to walk through.

Note: You may ask students to suggest additional things to walk through.

Take a Walk Suggestions

dust storm	thorny bushes	crowded concert
total darkness	super glue	snow storm
mashed potatoes	hot lava	river rapids
bubble gum	banana peels	feathers
center of the earth	tickle machine	marbles

Objective: Create imaginary environments through different movements.

⟷ Body Moving

How to play

❶ Start with students lined up, ready to act across the room.

❷ Tell students they will cross the space moving their bodies in different ways.

❸ Select a way to cross the space using the suggestions below such as walking backwards.

❹ Students cross as suggested, for this example, walking backwards.

❺ Between each turn, ask students to line up, listening for the next instruction.

❻ Choose three or more movements for the class to perform.

Note: You may ask students suggest additional ways to cross.

Body Moving Suggestions

skipping	walking	jumping
running	baby stepping	walking backwards
slithering	sneaking	spinning
giant stepping	leaping	floating
dancing	marching	crawling

Objective: Increase physical fitness and limber up the body.

←→Without Words

How to play

❶Start with students lined up, ready to act across the room.

❷Tell students that they're going to cross the space performing without talking.

❸Select an action using the suggestions below such as riding a bike.

❹Students cross the space performing the suggested action, for this example, riding a bike.

❺Between each turn, ask students to line up, listening for the next instruction.

❻Choose three or more actions for the class to perform.

Note: You may ask students to suggest additional actions they would like to perform.

Without Words Suggestions

walking on the moon	crossing a street	paddling a kayak
planting a garden	hang gliding	as shooting stars
riding a bike	delivering mail	reading a comic book
gathering fire wood	crossing a stream	on a pogo stick

Objective: Expand student's knowledge of pantomime through performance.

←→Changing Environments

How to play

❶ Start with students lined up, ready to act across the room.

❷ Tell students they're going to cross the space experiencing different environments.

❸ Select an environment using the suggestions below such as on the beach.

❹ Students cross the space as suggested, for this example, on the beach.

❺ Between each turn, ask students to line up, listening for the next instruction.

❻ Choose three or more environments for the class to explore.

Note: You may ask students to discuss each environment before crossing the space. Students may also suggest environments.

Changing Environments Suggestions

an amusement park	a traffic jam	a far away galaxy
the desert	a secret passage	at the mall
a thick fog	a rainstorm	underwater
a windy day	a haunted house	a dance club
a school pep rally	a movie set	a chocolate factory

Objective: Use the imagination to discover different environments.

←→Emotion Crossing

How to play

❶Start with students lined up, ready to act across the space.

❷Tell students that they're going to cross the space performing an emotion. Explain that an emotion is the way you feel about something such as happy, sad, shy, or angry.

❸Select an emotion for the class to perform using the suggestions below such as excited.

❹Students cross the space performing the suggestion, for this example, excited.

❺Between each turn, ask students to line up, listening for the next instruction.

❻Choose three or more emotions for the class to perform.

Note: If students need guidance, discuss each emotion before the students cross the space or demonstrate for the class.

Emotion Crossing Suggestions

cheerful	miserable	snooping	furious
bashful	envious	stern	ridiculous
worried	suspicious	energized	unwell
stressed	dumbfounded	calm	dejected
hip	accommodating	anxious	shifty

Objective: Explore different emotions and feelings through dramatic play.

←→ Stages of Life

How to play

❶ Start with students lined up, ready to act.

❷ Tell students that they're going to perform the stages of life.

❸ Ask students about each stage of life using the dialog below.

❹ Ask a question and select a student to answer.

❺ Cross the space acting out each stage of life, and then ask students the next question.

❻ When all stages of life have been performed, the game is complete.

Stages of Life Dialog

Teacher: "What is the first thing that happens to you in life?"
Students: "You are born."
Teacher: "Right, let's cross the room as if we were just born."
Class crosses the space with teacher.

Teacher: "Then you begin to crawl, and you are called?"
Students: "Babies."
Teacher: "That's right, let's all cross the room as babies."
Class crosses the space with teacher – crawling.

Note: Remember to ask the class about each stage of life.
For example: What do babies do? or What do adults do?
This provides the class with ideas on how to cross the space.

Teacher: "After you're babies, you get bigger and you are…?"
Students: "Toddlers."
Teacher: "Yes, let's all cross like we're toddlers."
Class crosses the space with teacher – toddling.

Teacher: "Then after that, you get a little bigger, you are called?"
Students: "Kids."
Teacher: "That's right, let's all cross like we're kids."
Class crosses the space with teacher – playing.

Teacher: "After your kids, what is the next stage of life?"
Students: "Teenagers."
Teacher: "Yes, let's all cross like teenagers."
Class crosses the space with teacher – as teenagers.

Teacher: "Then you grow up even more, and you become?"
Students: "Adults."
Teacher: "That's right, let's all cross like adults."
Class crosses the space with teacher – as adults.

Teacher: "What is the next stage of life, after adults?"
Students: "Grandparents."
Teacher: "Yes, let's all cross like grandparents."
Class crosses the space with teacher – as grandparents.

Teacher: "We were born, we were babies, toddlers, kids, teenagers, adults, grandparents, and then what happens after that?"
Students: "You die."
Teacher: "That's right, let's all cross the space pretending to die."
Class crosses the space with teacher – dying.

Teacher: "Then what happens?"
Students: "You fly like angels."
Teachers: "Yes! Everyone fly around like angels."
Class crosses the space with teacher – flying.

Objectives: Increase knowledge of life's stages through acting and discussion.

←→Working with Animals

How to play

❶Start with students lined up, ready to act across the room.

❷Tell students that they're going to cross the space performing different actions with pretend animals.

❸Begin the game with students making the sounds of animals.

❹Select an action using the suggestions below such as riding on a camel.

❺Ask students to cross the space as suggested, for this example, riding on a camel.

❻Between each turn, ask students to line up, listening for the next instruction.

❼Choose three or more actions for the class to perform.

Working with Animals Suggestions

driving dogsleds	walking with seeing eye dogs
riding on elephants	riding horses
swimming with dolphins	taming lions
plowing with oxen	swinging on vines with monkeys
herding cattle	riding on whales

> *Objective: Explore and appreciate animal's work through imaginative play.*

←→Copy Cat

How to play

❶Start with students lined up, ready to act across the space.

❷Tell the class that they're going to cross the space copying the student who is leading.

❸Begin the game by asking students to copy your movements, and skip across the space as the class follows you.

❹Ask students to raise their hands when they're ready for a turn to lead.

Note: Tell students that they can speak or make sounds along with their movements.

❺Select a student to lead the class across the space. Remind everyone to copy the leader's movements and sounds as closely as possible.

❻When everyone has had a turn to lead the class, the game is complete.

Note: Encourage everyone to be polite to each other and they will be rewarded with a chance to lead the class.

Objective: Promote individuality, leadership, and politeness.

←→Greeting Game

How to play

❶Start by asking students to find a partner.

❷Ask students to form two lines on opposite sides of the space, with partners facing each other. Tell students that partners will greet each other in the center of the space, and cross to the opposite line.

❸Ask for a volunteer and demonstrate greeting each other in a friendly manner, then cross to the opposite side of the space (see the Greeting Game Formation below).

❹Instruct students to cross the space, greet their partner in a friendly manner, and then go to the opposite line.

❺Announce three or more greetings for pairs to perform using the suggestions on the following page, or mix and match them.

❻At the end of each turn, ask one pair of students to demonstrate the greeting for the class.

Note: You may ask students to suggest additional greetings for the class to perform.

Greeting Game Formation

Characters	Emotions	Actions
giants	cool	on motorcycles
ghosts	sadly	walking a dog
kings/queens	sleepy	floating on a cloud
soldiers	surprised	playing an instrument
aliens	in a hurry	hiccupping
little trolls	cold	picking flowers
little fish	excited	in slow motion
ballerinas	hungry	shooting a movie
secret agents	shy	limping
klutzes	silly	roller skating
karate masters	politely	jogging
scientists	frustrated	playing tag
babies	happy	dancing
rock climbers	peaceful	jumping rope
horseback riders	sneaky	looking for clues
clowns	laughing	skipping
robots	stubborn	break dancing
ninjas	sick	flying

Objective: Improve social skills by interacting with a partner in a variety of ways.

←→Emergencies

How to play

❶ Start with students lined up, ready to act across the room.

❷ Tell students they're going to cross the space performing in different emergency situations.

❸ Select an emergency using the suggestions below such as in an earthquake.

❹ Students act across the space, pretending to be involved in the emergency, for this example, in an earthquake.

Note: Encourage students to work together and help each other through the emergencies.

❺ Between each turn, ask students to line up, listening for the next instruction.

❻ Choose three or more emergencies for the class to perform.

Note: You may ask students to suggest additional emergencies to perform.

Emergencies Suggestions

tidal wave	forest fire	volcano erupting
flood	alien invasion	cat stuck in a tree
mudslide	sinking ship	hurricane
quicksand	avalanche	killer ants

Objective: Learn how to react in a situation that requires immediate attention.

←→Add-on

How to play

❶Start with students lined up, ready to act across the room.

❷Tell students that they will cross the space as different characters, however, each time they cross a new characteristic will be added.

❸Choose a character using the suggestions below such as aliens, and ask students to cross the space as suggested.

❹Students line up, and teacher announces Add-on #1 such as aliens with the hiccups.

❺Ask students to cross the space as suggested.

❻Students line up, and teacher announces Add-on #2 such as aliens with the hiccups, and a broken leg.

❼Students cross the space as suggested. Select three or more characters with Add-on's to perform.

Character	Add-on #1	Add-on #2
pirates	catching big fish	with poison ivy
mad scientists	with stomach aches	playing freeze tag
disco dancers	with itchy backs	need to use bathroom
jugglers	on skateboards	yodeling
gymnasts	catching leaves	sneezing
ghosts	snowboarding	singing opera

Objective: Improve acting and memory skills by incorporating multiple actions to characters.

⟷Action/Reaction

How to play

❶ Start with students lined up, ready to act.

❷ Tell students to cross the space like they're bumblebees.

❸ Ask students to line up, listening for the next instruction.

❹ Tell students to cross again as if bumblebees are chasing them.

❺ Select three or more scenarios using the suggestions below.

Note: You may ask students to create additional Action/Reaction suggestions.

Action/Reaction Suggestions

as giants/hiding from giants

as rabbits eating in a garden/as farmers chasing rabbits out of garden

swimming like sharks/swimming away from sharks

as dinosaurs stomping/as cave people running away from dinosaurs

putting out a fire/running from a fire

climbing up a mountain/falling down a mountain

Objective: Introduce students to acting and reacting to dramatic situations.

←→Slow Motion

How to play

❶ Start with students lined up, ready to act across the room.

❷ Tell students that they're going to perform in slow motion.

❸ Select an action for the class to perform using the suggestions below.

❹ Students cross the space in slow motion as suggested.

❺ Between each turn, ask students to line up, listening for the next instruction.

❻ Choose three or more slow motion actions for the class to perform.

Note: Between each action, you may ask one or two students to demonstrate in slow motion.

Slow Motion Suggestions

scoring the winning touchdown	grooving across the dance floor
tumbleweeds blowing	surfing wipe out
dribbling a basketball	knights jousting
crossing a finishing line	high five a friend
slipping on black ice	searching for water in the desert

Objective: Work on body control and timing through creative movement.

←→Character Crossing

How to play

❶ Start with students lined up, ready to act.

❷ Tell students that they're going to cross the space performing different characters.

❸ Choose a character for students to perform using the suggestions below such as little elves. Students cross the space as suggested.

❹ Between each turn, ask students to line up, listening for the next instruction.

❺ Have students cross as three or more characters.

Note: You may ask students to share additional character suggestions or make up your own.

Character Crossing Suggestions

little elves	game show hosts	scuba divers
astronauts	pizza chefs	nerds
sailors	bus drivers	movie stars
airplane pilots	tv news reporters	jesters
magicians	police officers	wizards
vampires	snake charmers	superheroes

Objective: Explore characters and artistic expression through movement.

Acting Games

Play-Ground Theatre Acting Games

Play-Ground Theatre Acting Games offer students an opportunity to share their creative expression, and sharpen their dramatic abilities in a supportive atmosphere. They teach students stage presence, line delivery, characterization, and cultivate self-confidence. During Acting Games, students who are not on stage represent the audience. This encourages politeness in the audience as it teaches students on stage how to entertain their peers.

To keep the students involved and courteous to the actors, you will use an animated and effective technique called, "AND ACTION!" Each time students perform, the audience is instructed to begin the scene with the phrase, "AND ACTION!" Demonstrate this by swinging the arm forward, and pointing the index finger to the stage area.

<u>Acting Games Included:</u>

Actor and Audience	Opening Line
Can I Help You?	English/Gibberish
Pajama Party	Entrance Game
All Together Now	Theme Scenes
Age Game	Language Barriers
Commercials	Phone Game
Scenes in a Hat	Role Reversal
The Secret	

Acting Game ★ Instructions

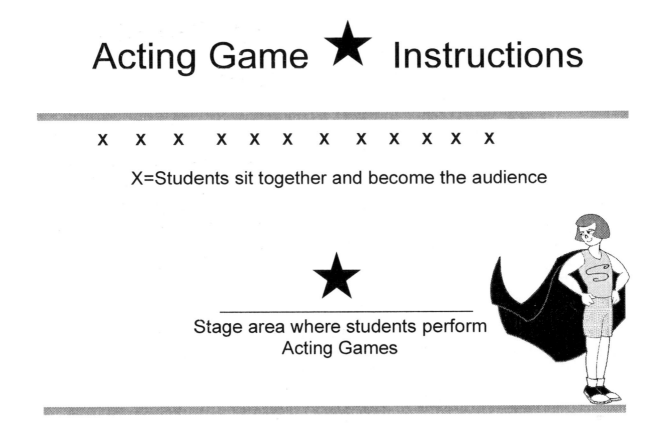

x x x x x x x x x x x

X=Students sit together and become the audience

★
_____
Stage area where students perform
Acting Games

❶ Start with students sitting to form an audience.

❷ Teacher gives instructions, and goes over the stage rules:

- Always face the audience.
- Speak clearly and in a nice, loud voice.
- Have fun on stage!

❸ Remind students in the audience to be polite and quiet.

❹ Begin each turn with the line, "AND ACTION!"

❺ Students take turns performing for each other.

★ Actor and Audience

How to play

❶Start by dividing the class in half. Ask half the class to sit down to form the audience, and the other half to stand up on the stage to become the actors.

❷Ask the actors to enter the stage, face the audience and say, "Hello audience!" Tell the audience to respond by saying, "Hello actors!"

❸Select an action for the actors to perform using the suggestions below. Start by having the class say, "AND ACTION!"

❹After a few moments, instruct the actors to "FREEZE!" and select a different action to perform. Start again by saying, "AND ACTION!"

❺Actors on stage perform three or more actions, then bow as the audience applauds.

❻Switch the groups, so the students in the audience become the actors on stage, and begin again.

Actor and Audience Suggestions

lifting 10,000lbs	taking a test	aliens landing
sleep walking	eating ice cream	collecting fossils
trapped in elevator	lying on the beach	brushing a horse
dancing a jig	playing a video game	making lunch
catching a fly ball	fixing a flat tire	looking in a telescope
playing a violin	painting a picture	learning to drive

Objective: Introduce audience participation and fundamental acting skills.

 Opening Line

How to play

❶ Tell the class that they're going to perform a scene with a partner, and you will give them the opening line.

❷ Choose two students to perform a scene.

❸ Give students a situation and a first line using the suggestions below. Select a student to deliver the first line.

❹ Have the class begin each scene by saying, "AND ACTION!"

Scene	First Line
on a hike	"How much further is it, I'm getting tired?"
babysitting	"Okay, that's enough of that. It's time for bed."
on a pirate ship	"Arrrrrrr matie! Where's the treasure map?"
at the senior center	"Speak up sonny, I can hear a thing!"
teenager party	"Check it out, I just got my drivers license!"
in the hospital	"The operation was a complete success."
principal's office	"We need to talk to about your behavior."
at the bus stop	"Do you smell that?"
in gym class	"Uh oh, I think I just hurt myself."
on the playground	"I bet you can't do this."
at the movies	"This is too scary. I can't watch!"

Objective: Working with partner to hone improvisation skills.

★ Can I Help You?

How to play

❶ Ask students to find a partner and sit down for instructions.

❷ Tell students that they're going to perform a scene where the intention is to cooperate with each other.

❸ Ask students to raise their hands when ready to perform, and choose a pair to take the stage. Select an action using the suggestions below, and announce it to the class. Begin each turn by saying, "AND ACTION!"

❹ The scene begins with one student performing the action, after a few moments, the second student enters and finds his/her friend hard at work. The second student says, "Can I help you?" and the action is completed together.

❺ Select a new pair of students to take the stage, choose a different action to perform, and begin again.

❻ When everyone has had a turn, the game is complete.

Can I Help You Suggestions

sweeping the floor	making a bed	cleaning the bathroom
raking leaves	peeling potatoes	weeding a garden
cutting the lawn	taking out trash	feeding a pet
rehearsing lines	fixing a bird house	putting away groceries

Objective: Connecting to good-natured behavior through role playing.

 English/Gibberish

How to play

❶ Start with students finding a partner and sitting for instructions.

❷ Tell students that they're going to perform a scene speaking in English, and then speaking in their own gibberish language.

❸ Select the first pair to perform, and announce a situation using the suggestions below. Audience says, "AND ACTION!" actors begin speaking in English.

❹ After a few moments the teacher says, "SWITCH," and the scene turns from speaking English to speaking gibberish.

❺ As the scene continues, teacher says, "SWITCH" again, and the scene returns to English. Switch three or more times per scene.

❻ Ask students to bow and sit down as the audience claps, then select the next pair to perform. When everyone has had a turn, the game is complete.

English/Gibberish Suggestions

Television hosts in the studio, introducing a fast paced sports show.

Vendors on the street of an outdoor fish market.

Scientists in a lab discovering the cure for a rare disease.

Football players at half time psyched up to win the big game.

Parents at dinner discussing where to take the family on vacation.

Teachers in a meeting talking about a new achievement test.

Objective: Strengthen comic abilities by creating your own language and gestures.

 Pajama Party

How to play

❶Start with students sitting down for instructions.

❷Tell students that they're going to play a guessing game called Pajama Party.

❸Select a student to host the party. He/she will try to guess who is attending the party at the end of the scene.

❹Select three students to attend the party, and secretly give each student a character identity using the suggestions on the following page.

❺Begin the scene by saying, "AND ACTION!" The host is alone on stage, getting ready for the guests to arrive.

❻Teacher instructs the audience to ring the doorbell, "Ding Dong." The first guest enters the party, in character, and talks with the host.

❼The doorbell rings again, and the second guest enters, in character, and is greeted by the host.

❽After a few moments, the doorbell rings again, and the third guest enters, in character, and is greeted by the host. The actors continue the scene until the host is ready to guess who they are.

❾The host makes a guess. If the guess is correct, that character bows and exits. If the guess is incorrect, the scene continues until the identity is revealed.

❿When each character has been identified, select a new host, three characters, and begin again.

Pajama Party Character Suggestions

Easter bunny	car salesman
wicked witch	leprechaun
psychic	comedian
angel	devil
big bad wolf	Little Miss Muffet
prince charming	Cleopatra
Miss America	pirate captain
army general	Cinderella
lifeguard	dentist
big foot	president
yoga instructor	Little Red Riding Hood
Frankenstein	Santa Claus
lumberjack	magical unicorn
little old lady	hair dresser
mean troll	gold miner
baby genius	rapper
baseball umpire	hippie
cupid	sandman
computer geek	Gingerbread Man
magic genie	homeless person
pro wrestler	horse whisperer
ice cream vendor	park ranger

Objective: Portraying characters in a scene, interacting with four actors on stage.

★ Entrance Game

How to play

❶Start with students finding a partner, and sitting for instructions.

❷Each pair is given an entrance to perform using the suggestions below. This must be kept secret from the audience.

❸Students raise their hands when they are ready for a turn.

❹Select the first pair of students, and quietly instruct them on how to enter the stage. Make sure the class does not hear.

❺Students in the audience give actors the cue, "AND ACTION!" to begin each turn.

❻The actors enter as instructed, after a few moments, the "FREEZE!" cue is given, and the audience guesses the action.

❼When the correct answer is given, ask students on stage to bow, audience applauds, and the next pair has a turn.

❽After each pair has had a turn, the game is complete.

Entrance Game Suggestions

looking for treasure	climbing a mountain	swimming
hitting a home run	walking a big dog	playing guitars
making a snowman	tight rope walkers	washing a car
building a tree house	making breakfast	camping

Objective: Communicate an action while entering the stage with a partner.

★ All Together Now

How to play

❶ Start with students sitting down for instructions.

❷ Tell students that they're going to act out different things together.

❸ Ask students to perform an action together using the suggestions below such as playing in an orchestra.

❹ When everyone is ready to begin, students are instructed to say, "AND ACTION!"

❺ The class performs the scene for a few moments, until the "FREEZE!" cue is given, and a new action is selected.

❻ Select three or more actions for the class to perform.

Note: If you have two teachers, try this activity as a guessing game. Teacher one leaves the room. The second teacher selects and performs the suggestion with the class. Teacher one returns and guesses the action.

All Together Now Suggestions

a school of fish	sea turtles swimming	washing machine
a vase of flowers	bacon sizzling	bees in a hive
cheerleaders	a thunder cloud	a river
trick or treating	a bridge	chickens laying eggs

Objective: Perform a short scene with the entire class.

 # ★ Theme Scenes

How to play

❶ Ask students to find a partner and sit down for instructions.

❷ Tell students that they're going to perform scenes using different themes. When students are ready, select the first pair to go on stage.

❸ Select a scene title and a theme using the suggestions on the following page such as "the lunch break" with the theme talk show.

❹ Begin the scene by saying, "AND ACTION!" After a few moments of performing, instruct the students to "FREEZE!"

❺ Change the theme of the scene to a cartoon, and resume the scene. For this example, students perform "the lunch break" as a cartoon.

❻ After a few moments, instruct the students to "FREEZE!" Switch the themes back and forth three or more times.

❼ At the end of the scene, the students bow as the audience claps.

❽ Select another pair to perform, and begin a new scene.

❾ When everyone has had a chance to perform, the game is complete.

Note: If students need help with the theme suggestions, demonstrate the acting style before beginning the scene. You may ask students to suggest additional themes or situations.

Theme Scenes Suggestions	Themes
the birthday party	soap opera
the wedding	children's show
the break up	horror movie
long lost friends	mystery theatre
graduation day	cartoon
the broken down car	talk show
ice fishing in the artic	Broadway musical
summer camp	silent movie
the missed flight	sit com
moving day misadventures	action/adventure
the best vacation ever	radio play
archeologists on a dig	science fiction
the new puppy	documentary
family feud	news report
the dragons kingdom	police show
a trip to the moon	after school special
midnight train to Memphis	drama

Objective: Compare presentation styles and their effects on the actors and audience.

 # Age Game

How to play

❶ Start with students finding a partner and sitting for instructions.

❷ Tell students that each pair must choose the same age to perform, between one and one hundred years, this age must be kept secret.

❸ Pairs that are ready raise their hands. Ask each pair of actors to whisper their age to you, before the scene begins.

❹ Begin each turn by saying, "AND ACTION!" Allow each pair to act for a few moments then say, "FREEZE!"

❺ Ask students in the audience to raise their hands to guess the age being performed. If the correct age is higher than the age guessed, tell the class, "higher." If the correct age is lower than the age guessed, tell the class, "lower."

❻ When the correct age is guessed, actors bow, the audience applauds, and the next pair has a turn.

Note: Each pair performs a short scene, so remind the audience to remain quiet and polite until the "FREEZE!" cue is given.

❼ After each pair has had a turn, ask to students switch partners, choose a new age, and begin again.

Objective: Gain an understanding of different ages through performance.

★ Language Barriers

How to play

❶Ask students to sit down to form the audience.

❷Tell students that they're going to portray people from a non-English speaking country. The student performing will be from the United States, and need something from the audience, which is described through pantomime.

❸Select a student and ask him/her to announce a country for the audience to represent such as France.

❹Whisper the item the student will need to ask for using the suggestions below such as a band-aid.

❺Begin the scene by saying, "AND ACTION!"

❻Student performs pantomime, asking the audience for the suggested item, in this example, for a band-aid.

❼Select students to guess what is being asked for. When the correct answer is given, the actor bows, and a new student has a turn.

❽When everyone has had a turn, the game is complete.

Language Barrier Suggestions

toothbrush	sunglasses	cup of coffee	shampoo
aspirin	lost luggage	toilet plunger	light bulb
cheese pizza	taxi cab	subway train	telephone

Objective: Communicate with pantomime and hone individual stage skills.

★ Commercials

Materials

props - one for each student playing

How to play

❶Start with students sitting down for instructions.

❷Tell students that they're going to create their own commercials, for products, which you will give them.

❸Give each student a prop for his/her commercial. Tell students that their commercials should include: a product name, what the product does, where to get it, and how much it costs.

❹Allow a few minutes for students to create their commercials.

Note: Check in with students to make sure they feel confident, and answer any questions they may have.

❺Select a student to perform his/her commercial. Begin by saying, "AND ACTION!" Student performs commercial for thirty seconds.

❻Select students, one at a time, to perform for the class.

❼After each student has a turn to perform, the game is complete.

Note: You may try this as a movie trailer game, where student groups create coming attractions for original films.

Objective: Polish improvisation skills, foster individuality, and creative style.

★ Phone Game

Materials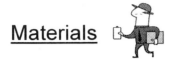

toy or old telephone

How to play

❶ Start with students sitting down for instructions. Tell students that they're going to take turns pretending to talk on the phone.

❷ Ask students to raise their hands when they're ready for a turn.

❸ Select a student and tell him/her who is calling using the suggestions below. Ask the audience to ring the phone three times, before the student answers.

❹ The student says, "Hello?" then performs a short conversation. At the end of the call, the student says, "Thanks for calling. Bye." Finally, the student hangs up the phone.

❺ When everyone has had a turn, the game is complete.

Phone Game Suggestions

dad is calling	sheriff is calling	teacher is calling
best friend is calling	mom is calling	President is calling
movie star is calling	alien is calling	dentist is calling
grandma is calling	Santa is calling	principal is calling

Objective: Learn phone conversation and communication skills.

★ Scenes in a Hat

Materials

a hat
Scenes in a Hat Suggestions (see next page)

How to play

❶ Copy, cut, and place suggestions inside the hat.

❷ Ask students to sit down and listen to instructions.

❸ Tell students they will have a chance to pick a scene title from the hat.

❹ Select two students to perform and have them pick one scene title from the hat.

❺ Teacher announces the scene title for the to students perform. Begin the scene by saying, "AND ACTION!"

❻ When the scene is complete, select another pair to pick from the hat.

❼ When everyone has had a turn, the game is complete.

Note: You may allow extra time for students to create their scenes. Students may write down additional scene titles to pull from the hat.

Objective: Develop acting skills and share talents with others.

Scenes in a Hat Suggestions – copy, cut and place in hat.

Tooth Fairy Diaries	The Pie Eating Contest
The Fortune Teller	The Midnight Burglars
The Ice Show	Adventures in Outer Space
The Missing Birthday Present	A Visit to Grandpa's House
Lost in the Cave	The Secret Meeting
The Worm Farm	The Great Invention
Mystery Under the Sea	The Runaway
A Day in the Life of a Superhero	The Noisy Neighbor
Stranded on Ghoul Island	The Shipwreck
The Good Deed	The Basketball Blunder

 Role Reversal

How to play

❶ Start with students sitting down for instructions.

❷ Tell students that they're going to play Role Reversal.

❸ Select two students and assign them parts using the suggestions below such as parent/child, then give them the situation.

❹ Begin the scene by saying, "AND ACTION!" and students perform. After a few moments, the "FREEZE!" cue is given.

❺ Tell students to switch roles. For this example, the child becomes the parent, and the parent is the child.

❻ Begin again by saying, "AND ACTION"! After a few more moments, the "FREEZE!" cue is given, and the actors bow and sit down.

❼ Select two students and begin again with new characters and situation. When everyone has had a turn, the game is complete.

Role Reversal Suggestions   Situations

teacher/student	having a conference about bad grades
rock star/groupie	autographing t-shirts after concert
coach/athlete	discussing strategy for championship
parent/child	discussing curfew
gardener/gopher	discovering holes in garden
superhero/villain	struggle to save the world
customer/wait staff	complaint over wrong order
actor/agent	negotiating movie contract

Objective: Understanding both sides of every situation.

 # The Secret

How to play

❶ Ask students to choose a partner and sit down for instructions.

❷ Tell students that they're going to perform a scene in which each actor will reveal a secret.

❸ Select a pair and give them situation using the suggestions below such as witches discussing a secret brew ingredient.

❹ Begin the scene by saying, "AND ACTION!" Students perform as suggested and reveal a secret during the scene.

❺ After a few moments, ask students to wrap up the scene and exit.

❻ Select the next pair and give them a new situation. When everyone has had a turn, the game is complete.

The Secret Suggestions

kids in a club house making up a secret knock

business executives working on a secret project

girls on the phone talking about a secret crush

international spies meeting at a secret hideout

gossiping neighbors talking at the school bus stop

parents planning a sweet sixteen surprise party

little league coaches discussing the upcoming draft

Objective: Challenge improvisational skills by adding secret objectives.

Play-Ground Theatre

Part Two

Theatre Games for Elementary School Children Ages 7-12

Create Characters, Lines, Scenes, Scripts & Songs

Create Characters, Lines, Scenes, Scripts & Songs Instructions

This section includes fifteen characters designed for creative exploration. Each character offers four worksheets for you to copy and hand out.

Worksheets aid students to invent their own characters, create lines, develop scenes, and finally write scripts or songs. Students may also craft dance choreography, work on costume designs, draw pictures, or perform their ideas for the full creative experience. Worksheets include:

❶ Meet the Character

❷ Create your own Character

❸ Create your own Lines & Scenes

❹ Create Scripts, Songs, or Works of Art

Note: For younger actors, teachers may want to guide students by reading the examples aloud, and filling in the worksheets as a group exercise. Then ask students to perform their character ideas.

Lights, camera, action! Stimulate your students with theatre activities that invite them to share their individual ideas. Worksheets include easy-to-follow instructions to motivate students, increase literacy, and aid teachers in their quest to provide quality children's theatre.

www.playgroundtheatre.com

Play-Ground Theatre Characters

Mad Scientist

Rock Star

Super Hero

Cowboy

Alien

Clown

Robot

Farmer

Secret Agent

Ballet Dancer

Wizard

Pirate

Mermaid

Knight

Ghost

Meet the Mad Scientist

Create your own Mad Scientist

Answer the questions below to invent your own Mad Scientist.

❶What is your Mad Scientist's Name?
Example: My mad scientist's name is Doctor Big Brain.

_____

❷What kind of costume does your Mad Scientist wear?
Example: Doctor Big Brain has bright red hair, wears goggles, a labcoat, and purple high top sneakers.

_____

❸Where does your Mad Scientist live?
Example: Doctor Big Brain lives in a castle, in Germany.

_____

❹What does your Mad Scientist do?
Example: Doctor Big Brain invents the first invisibility potion.

_____

❺Does your Mad Scientist speak with an accent? If yes, what kind? Example: Yes, Doctor Big Brain speaks in a thick German accent, and has a loud, crazy laugh.

_____

❻Who are your Mad Scientist's friends?
Example: Doctor Big Brain's best friend is his trusty assistant Igor.

_____

❼Does your Mad Scientist have any special abilities or powers?
Example: Doctor Big Brain is a math genuis, and has highest IQ in the world.

 # Create your own Lines & Scenes

In the space below, invent lines and scenes for your Mad Scientist.

Lines for your Mad Scientist:

Example: "It's time to test my invisibility potion. Quickly Igor, I need your help!"

1. _____

2. _____

3. _____

4. _____

5. _____

Scenes for your Mad Scientist:

Example: (1) meet Doctor Big Brain and his assistant Igor (2) create invisibility potion in the secret laboratory (3) test the potion on Igor (4) potion backfires (5) hide and seek with Igor and Doctor Big Brain (6) fix the potion with special ingredient (7) potion works, Doctor Big Brain and Igor celebrate

1. _____

2. _____

3. _____

4. _____

5. _____

6. _____

7. _____

Mad Scientist - Script, Song, or Work of Art

In the space below, write a script, song, story, rap, or dance moves. On a separate piece of paper, you may design a costume or draw a picture of your Mad Scientist.

Title:_____

_____

_____

_____

_____

_____

_____

_____

_____

_____

_____

_____

_____

_____

_____

_____

_____

_____

_____

_____

_____

Written by:_____

Meet the Rock Star

www.playgroundtheatre.com

Create your own Rock Star

Answer the questions below to invent your own Rock Star.

❶What is your Rock Star's Name?
Example: My rock star's name is Flash.

_____

❷What kind of costume does your Rock Star wear?
Example: Flash wears sun glasses, flashy clothes, and plays a red electric guitar.

_____

❸Where does your Rock Star live?
Example: Flash was born in London, but now lives in Los Angeles.

_____

❹What does your Rock Star do?
Example: Flash travels around the world performing for millions of fans.

_____

❺Does your Rock Star speak with an accent? If yes, what kind?
Example: Yes, Flash speaks with a British accent.

_____

❻Who are your Rock Star's friends?
Example: Flash hangs out with his band, manager, and groupies.

_____

❼Does your Rock Star have any special abilities or powers?
Example: Flash is in the Rock and Roll Hall of Fame.

_____

# Create your own Lines & Scenes

In the space below, create lines and scenes for your Rock Star.

Lines for your Rock Star:
Example: "Last night's concert was brilliant. The crowd was completely electric!"

1. _____

2. _____

3. _____

4. _____

5. _____

Scenes for your Rock Star:
Example: (1) meet Flash and his band (2) band flys to New York City for a sold out concert (3) fans get autographs (4) press conference with news reporters (5) back stage with band before the show (6) the concert rocks (7) music video out

1. _____

2. _____

3. _____

4. _____

5. _____

6. _____

7. _____

Rock Star - Script, Song, or Work of Art

In the space below, write a script, song, story, rap, or dance moves.
On a separate piece of paper, you may design a costume or
draw a picture of your Rock Star.

Name:_____

_____

_____

_____

_____

_____

_____

_____

_____

_____

_____

_____

_____

_____

_____

_____

_____

_____

_____

_____

Written by:_____

Meet the Superhero

Create your own Superhero

Answer the questions below to invent your own Superhero.

❶What is your Superhero's Name?
Example: My superhero's name is Solar Star.

_____

❷What kind of costume does your Superhero wear?
Example: Solar Star wears a long flowing cape.

_____

❸Where does your Superhero live?
Example: Solar Star lives on a secret island off the Florida Keys.

_____

❹What does your Superhero do?
Example: Solar Star dedicates her life to helping others, and keeping the world safe for everyone.

_____

❺Does your Superhero speak with an accent? If yes, what kind?
Example: Solar Star speaks with an accent that is unique to her island.

_____

❻Who are your Superhero's friends?
Example: Solar Star has a dolphin friend named Dannie.

_____

❼Does your Superhero have any special abilities or powers?
Example: Solar Star has great strength, she can fly, and speak to animals.

_____

# Create your own Lines & Scenes

In the space below, create lines and scenes for your Superhero.

Lines for your Superhero:
Example: "Don't worry Dannie, we can stop that boat from sinking!"

1. _____

2. _____

3. _____

4. _____

5. _____

Scenes for your Superhero:
Example: (1) meet Solar Star and her sidekick Dannie the dolphin (2) Dannie senses trouble, a boat is sinking (3) Solar Star rescues boat passengers (4) Solar Star and Dannie investigate lagoon (5) a family of baby loons are trapped (6) Solar Star to the rescue (7) Solar Star and Dannie watch the full moon rise

1. _____

2. _____

3. _____

4. _____

5. _____

6. _____

7. _____

Superhero - Script, Song, or Work of Art

In the space below, write a script, song, story, rap, or dance moves. On a separate piece of paper, you may design a costume or draw a picture of your Superhero.

Name:_____

_____

_____

_____

_____

_____

_____

_____

_____

_____

_____

_____

_____

_____

_____

_____

_____

_____

_____

_____

Written by:_____

Meet the Cowboy

www.playgroundtheatre.com

Create your own Cowboy

Answer the questions below to invent your own Cowboy.

❶What is your Cowboy's Name?
Example: My cowboy's name is Sheriff Spaghetti Pants.

_____

❷What kind of costume does your Cowboy wear?
Example: Sheriff Spaghetti Pants wears a big stetson, black chaps, a vest, a badge, and carries a lariat.

_____

❸Where does your Cowboy live?
Example: Sheriff Spaghetti Pants lives in Moon Gulch, Colorado.

_____

❹What does your Cowboy do?
Example: Sheriff Spaghetti Pants serves and protects the people in his town.

_____

❺Does your Cowboy speak with an accent? If yes, what kind?
Example: Yes, Sheriff Spaghetti Pants has a western accent.

_____

❻Who are your Cowboy's friends?
Example: The Sheriff's best friend is his deputy Dusty.

_____

❼Does your Cowboy have any special abilities or powers?
Example: The Sheriff's riding and roping is the best in the west.

_____

Create your own Lines & Scenes

In the space below, create lines and scenes for your Cowboy.

Lines for your Cowboy:

Example: "Howdy Partners! I'm the law in these here parts, so if you need help, just gimme a holler."

1. _____

2. _____

3. _____

4. _____

5. _____

Scenes for your Cowboy:

Example: (1) meet Sheriff Spaghetti Pants (2) Sheriff and deputy Dusty discover rash of crime by the Snatcher (3) Sheriff and Dusty set a trap for the Snatcher (4) Dusty falls asleep, and the Snatcher steals gold (5) Sheriff sets second trap (6) Sheriff catches Snatcher and puts him in jail (7) Sheriff and Dusty ride into the sunset

1. _____

2. _____

3. _____

4. _____

5. _____

6. _____

7. _____

Cowboy - Script, Song, or Work of Art

In the space below, write a script, song, story, rap, or dance moves. On a separate piece of paper, you may design a costume or draw a picture of your Cowboy.

Name:_____

_____

_____

_____

_____

_____

_____

_____

_____

_____

_____

_____

_____

_____

_____

_____

_____

_____

_____

_____

Written by:_____

Meet the Alien

Create your own Alien

Answer the questions below to invent your own Alien.

❶What is your Alien's Name?
Example: My alien's name is ZeeBop.

_____

❷What kind of costume does your Alien wear?
Example: ZeeBop wears a metalic jumpsuit, black cape, boots, tights, and a futuristic helmet.

_____

❸Where does your Alien live?
Example: ZeeBop is from the planet Zee.

_____

❹What does your Alien do?
Example: ZeeBop travels the universe exploring different life forms.

_____

❺Does your Alien speak with an accent? If yes, what kind?
Example: Yes, ZeeBop speaks with buzzes and beeps using fragmented English.

_____

❻Who are your Alien's friends?
Example: ZeeBop likes to make friends everybody.

_____

❼Does your Alien have any special abilities or powers?
Example: ZeeBop can dematerialize and rematerialize anywhere, anytime.

_____

Create your own Lines & Scenes

In the space below, create lines and scenes for your Alien.

Lines for your Alien:

Example: "Buzz, don't be, buzzbeep, afraid. I, buzzbeep, am your friend, Zeebop."

1. _____

2. _____

3. _____

4. _____

5. _____

Scenes for your Alien:

Example: (1) meet Zeebop flying in spaceship (2) Zeebop lands on the Earth's surface (3) Zeebop explores and meets an earthling (4) Zeebop gives the earthling a magic jewel from planet Zee (5) Zeebop is invited to dinner (6) Zeebop goes back to ship (7) blasts off into outer space until next adventure

1. _____

2. _____

3. _____

4. _____

5. _____

6. _____

7. _____

Alien - Script, Song, or Work of Art

In the space below, write a script, song, story, rap, or dance moves.
On a separate piece of paper, you may design a costume or
draw a picture of your Alien.

Name:_____

_____

_____

_____

_____

_____

_____

_____

_____

_____

_____

_____

_____

_____

_____

_____

_____

_____

_____

_____

_____

Written by:_____

Meet the Clown

www.playgroundtheatre.com

Create your own Clown

Answer the questions below and create your own Clown.

❶What is your Clown's Name?
Example: My clown's name is Zappy.

_____

❷What kind of costume does your Clown wear?
Example: Zappy wears big shoes, red and white stripe pants, a bow tie, and suspenders.

_____

❸Where does your Clown live?
Example: Zappy lives in Melbourne, Austraila.

_____

❹What does your Clown do?
Example: Zappy Is founder and President of Zappy's Little Circus, LLC.

_____

❺Does your Clown speak with an accent? If yes, what kind?
Example: Zappy speaks with a high, squeeky, Austrailian accent.

_____

❻Who are your Clown's friends?
Example: Zappy's best friend is Cyle the Crocodile.

_____

❼Does your Clown have any special abilities or powers?
Example: Zappy can juggle, and ride a miniture tricycle through a ring of fire.

_____

 # Create your own Lines & Scenes

In the space below, create lines and scenes for your Clown.

Lines for your Clown:

Example: "G'day mates, welcome to Zappy's Little Circus!"

1. _____

2. _____

3. _____

4. _____

5. _____

Scenes for your Clown:

Example: (1) meet Zappy graduating from clown college (2) Zappy and best friend, Cyle the Crocodile make plans to launch circus (3) auditions for Zappy's Little Circus (4) Cyle rehearses his trick on the high dive (5) Cyle gets stuck in bucket of water (6) circus performers work together to get Cyle free (7) Zappy build's Cyle a new bucket for the show

1. _____

2. _____

3. _____

4. _____

5. _____

6. _____

7. _____

Clown - Script, Song, or Work of Art

In the space below, write a script, song, story, rap, or dance moves.
On a separate piece of paper, you may design a costume or
draw a picture of your Clown.

Name:_____

_____

_____

_____

_____

_____

_____

_____

_____

_____

_____

_____

_____

_____

_____

_____

_____

_____

_____

_____

Written by:_____

Meet the Robot

Create your own Robot

Answer the questions below to invent your own Robot.

❶What is your Robot's Name?
Example: My robot's name is Power-Tron.

_____

❷What kind of costume does your Robot wear?
Example: Power-Tron wears a tin suit and has a silver face.

_____

❸Where does your Robot live?
Example: Power-Tron was created in a futuristic laboratory in Japan.

_____

❹What does your Robot do?
Example: Power-Tron is programed to solve world problems.

_____

❺Does your Robot speak with an accent? If yes, what kind?
Example: Power-Tron is programed to speak any language.

_____

❻Who are your Robot's friends?
Example: Power-Tron is friends with Mac the computer and his creator, Dr. Noodlefish.

_____

❼Does your Robot have any special abilities or powers?
Example: Power-Tron has super stregnth, speed, and brain functions.

_____

Create your own Lines & Scenes

In the space below, create lines and scenes for your Robot.

Lines for your Robot:

Example: "Hello, I am Power-Tron. I am programed to assist you."

1. _____

2. _____

3. _____

4. _____

5. _____

Scenes for your Robot:

Example: (1) meet Power-Tron (2) Power-Tron at the lab of Dr. Noodlefish (3) earthquake takes place
(4) Power-Tron gets assignment (5) aftermath of earthquake (5) Power-Tron resuces people from collapsed
bridge (6) Power-Tron is awarded a medal of bravery (7) Power-Tron and Dr. Noodlefish back in laboratory

1. _____

2. _____

3. _____

4. _____

5. _____

6. _____

7. _____

Robot - Script, Song, or Work of Art

In the space below, write a script, song, story, rap, or dance moves.
On a separate piece of paper, you may design a costume or
draw a picture of your Robot.

Name:_____

_____

_____

_____

_____

_____

_____

_____

_____

_____

_____

_____

_____

_____

_____

_____

_____

_____

_____

_____

_____

Written by:_____

Meet the Farmer

Create your own Farmer

Answer the questions below to invent your own Farmer.

❶What is your Farmer's Name?
Example: My farmer's name is Franny.

_____

❷What kind of costume does your Farmer wear?
Example: Franny wears overalls and a straw hat.

_____

❸Where does your Farmer live?
Example: Franny lives in Savannah, Georgia.

_____

❹What does your Farmer do?
Example. Franny works hard on her farm growing organic vetables.

_____

❺Does your Farmer speak with an accent? If yes, what kind?
Example: Yes, Franny speaks with a southern accent.

_____

❻Who are your Farmer's friends?
Example: Franny is friends with her neighbor, farmer McGreggor.

_____

❼Does your Farmer have any special abilities or powers?
Example: Franny's vegtables win blue ribbons at the state fair every year.

_____

 # Create your own Lines & Scenes

In the space below, create lines and scenes for your Farmer.

Lines for your Farmer:

Example: "Darlin, my secret's in the soil."

1. _____

2. _____

3. _____

4. _____

5. _____

Scenes for your Farmer:

Example: (1) meet Franny (2) Franny is getting ready for the state fair (3) Franny at the fair says hello to friends and fellow farmers (4) Franny wins the blue ribbon for her strawberry jam (5) Franny at home placing blue ribbon on her mantel (6) neighbor and friend, farmer McGreggor pays Franny a visit (7) Franny and farmer McGreggor have a piece of pie on the front porch, and laugh about old times

1. _____

2. _____

3. _____

4. _____

5. _____

6. _____

7. _____

Farmer - Script, Song, or Work of Art

In the space below, write a script, song, story, rap, or dance moves. On a separate piece of paper, you may design a costume or draw a picture of your Farmer.

Name:_____

_____

_____

_____

_____

_____

_____

_____

_____

_____

_____

_____

_____

_____

_____

_____

_____

_____

_____

_____

Written by:_____

Meet the Secret Agent

www.playgroundtheatre.com

Create your own Secret Agent

Answer the questions below to invent your own Secret Agent.

❶What is your Secret Agent's Name?
Example: My secret agent's name is Mr. X.

_____

❷What kind of costume does your Secret Agent wear?
Example: Mr X. wears a long trench coat, wide brim hat, and carries a brief case.

_____

❸Where does your Secret Agent live?
Example: Mr.X has a secret hide out, whereabouts unknown.

_____

❹What does your Secret Agent do?
Example: Mr. X breaks up and debunks criminal plots.

_____

❺Does your Secret Agent speak with an accent? If yes, what kind? Example: Mr. X can disguise his voice with many different accents.

_____

❻Who are your Secret Agent's friends?
Example: Mr. X trusts no one, he lives and works alone.

_____

❼Does your Secret Agent have any special abilities or powers?
Example: Mr. X carries a variety of gadgets that give him super advantages.

_____

# Create your own Lines & Scenes

In the space below, create lines and scenes for your Secret Agent.

Lines for your Secret Agent:

Example: "Another mystery solved by Mr. X."

1. _____

2. _____

3. _____

4. _____

5. _____

Scenes for your Secret Agent:

Example: (1) meet Mr. X (2) Mr. X drives in sports car (3) meeting with underground network (4) Mr. X gets orders (5) Mr. X meets Mr. Mustache at secret location (6) Mr. X foils the evil plans of Mr. Mustache (7) Mr. X rides away in sports car

1. _____

2. _____

3. _____

4. _____

5. _____

6. _____

7. _____

Secret Agent - Script, Song, or Work of Art

In the space below, write a script, song, story, rap, or dance moves. On a separate piece of paper, you may design a costume or draw a picture of your Secret Agent.

Name:_____

_____

_____

_____

_____

_____

_____

_____

_____

_____

_____

_____

_____

_____

_____

_____

_____

_____

_____

_____

_____

_____

Written by:_____

Meet the Ballet Dancer

Create your own Ballet Dancer

Answer the questions below to create your own Ballet Dancer.

❶What is your Ballet Dancer's Name?
Example: My ballet dancer's name is Twinkle.

_____

❷What kind of costume does your Ballet Dancer wear?
Example: Twinkle wears a pink and black leotard, pink tights, and toe shoes.

_____

❸Where does your Ballet Dancer live?
Example: Twinkle was born in Paris, and moved to Seattle, Washington.

_____

❹What does your Ballet Dancer do?
Example: Founder of the Twinkle Toes Dance Company.

_____

❺Does your Ballet Dancer speak with an accent? If yes, what kind? Example: Yes, Twinkle speaks with a French accent.

_____

❻Who are your Ballet Dancer's friends?
Example: Twinkle is friends with fellow dancers, Natasha and Elza.

_____

❼Does your Ballet Dancer have any special abilities or powers?
Example: Twinkle is one of the greatest ballet dancers in the world.

_____

Create your own Lines & Scenes

In the space below, create lines and scenes for your Ballet Dancer.

Lines for your Ballet Dancer:

Example: "Come everyone, we need to rehearse."

1. _____

2. _____

3. _____

4. _____

5. _____

Scenes for your Ballet Dancer:

Example: (1) meet Twinkle at dance studio (2) meet dance company at dress rehearsal (3) Twinkle has injury and goes to doctor (4) Twinkle recoperates with friends, Natasha and Elza (5) back to rehearsal (6) dance company backstage warming up for show (7) Twinkle delivers a stellar performance

1. _____

2. _____

3. _____

4. _____

5. _____

6. _____

7. _____

Ballet Dancer - Script, Song, or Work of Art

In the space below, write a script, song, story, rap, or dance moves.
On a separate piece of paper, you may design a costume or
draw a picture of your Ballet Dancer.

Name:_____

_____

_____

_____

_____

_____

_____

_____

_____

_____

_____

_____

_____

_____

_____

_____

_____

_____

_____

_____

_____

_____

Written by:_____

Meet the Wizard

Create your own Wizard

Answer the questions below to invent your own Wizard.

❶What is your Wizard's Name?
Example: My wizard's name is Waldrip.

---

❷What kind of costume does your Wizard wear?
Example: Waldrip wears a long robe, has a grey beard, and carries a magical staff.

---

❸Where does your Wizard live?
Example: Waldrip lives in Edinborough, Scottland.

---

❹What does your Wizard do?
Example: Waldrip helps the King make decisions.

---

❺Does your Wizard speak with an accent? If yes, what kind?
Example: Yes, Waldrip speaks with a Scottish accent.

---

❻Who are your Wizard friends?
Example: Waldrip is friends with the wise owl and the King.

---

❼Does your Wizard have any special abilities or powers?
Example: Waldrip can conjure magic with his staff, and he is a powerful potion maker.

Create your own Lines & Scenes

In the space below, create lines and scenes for your Wizard.

Lines for your Wizard:
Example: "Ippity, bipity, bip, my name is Wizard Waldrip."

1. _____

2. _____

3. _____

4. _____

5. _____

Scenes for your Wizard:
Example: (1) meet Waldrip (2) Waldrip walks through the woods collecting ingredients for potions
(3) making the King's potion (4) potion stollen by Lord LaBraker (5) King sends out knights to hunt for potion
(6) Waldrip conjures spell to get potion back (7) King takes potion and grows strong

1. _____

2. _____

3. _____

4. _____

5. _____

6. _____

7. _____

Wizard - Script, Song, or Work of Art

In the space below, write a script, song, story, rap, or dance moves. On a separate piece of paper, you may design a costume or draw a picture of your Wizard.

Name:_____

_____

_____

_____

_____

_____

_____

_____

_____

_____

_____

_____

_____

_____

_____

_____

_____

_____

_____

_____

_____

Written by:_____

Meet the Pirate

Create your own Pirate

Answer the questions below to invent your own Pirate.

❶What's your Pirate's Name?
Example: My pirate's name is Captain Underwear.

_____

❷What kind of costume does your Pirate wear?
Example: Captain Underwear has a red vest, black boots, an eye patch, and bandana.

_____

❸Where does your Pirate live?
Example: Captain Underwear lives on his ship, and sails the seven seas.

_____

❹What does your Pirate do?
Example: Captain Underwear looks for treasure, and has exciting adventures.

_____

❺Does your Pirate speak with an accent? If yes, what kind?
Example: Yes, Captain Underwear has a rough and raspy pirate voice.

_____

❻Who are your Pirate's friends?
Example: Captain Underwear's best friend is his first mate, Long John Slipper.

_____

❼Does your Pirate have any special abilities or powers?
Example: The Captain is a great map reader, sword fighter, and he makes a great chowder.

_____

Create your own Lines & Scenes

In the space below, create lines and scenes for your Pirate.

Lines for your Pirate:

Example: "Shiver me timbers, would you look at all this treasure!"

1. _____

2. _____

3. _____

4. _____

5. _____

Scenes for your Pirate:

Example: (1) meet Captin Underwear on his pirate ship (2) meet first mate Long John Slipper (3) Captain and Slipper set sail with treasure map (4) ship lands at Treasure Island, Captain and Slipper follow the map (5) find treasure (6) split the treasure (7) celebrate on the ship with music and chowder

1. _____

2. _____

3. _____

4. _____

5. _____

6. _____

7. _____

Pirate - Script, Song, or Work of Art

In the space below, write a script, song, story, rap, or dance moves. On a separate piece of paper, you may design a costume or draw a picture of your Pirate.

Name:_____

_____

_____

_____

_____

_____

_____

_____

_____

_____

_____

_____

_____

_____

_____

_____

_____

_____

_____

_____

_____

Written by:_____

Meet the Mermaid

Create your own Mermaid

Answer the questions below to invent your own Mermaid

❶What's your Mermaid's name?
Example: My mermaid's name is Splash.

_____

❷What kind of costume does your Mermaid wear?
Example: Splash wears sea flowers in her hair, a bikini top, pearls, and has a green tail.

_____

❸Where does your Mermaid live?
Example: Splash lives under the sea in Atlantis.

_____

❹What does your Mermaid do?
Example: Splash plays with her friends and goes to school.

_____

❺Does your Mermaid speak with an accent? If yes, what kind?
Example: Splash has a fluttery, soft voice, and she speaks in rhyme.

_____

❻Who are your Mermaid's friends?
Example: Splash's mermaid friends are Coral, Crystal, and Kelp.

_____

❼Does your Mermaid have any special abilities or powers?
Example: Splash is the fastest swimmer in Atlantis.

_____

 # Create your own Lines & Scenes

In the space below, create lines and scenes for your Mermaid.

Lines for your Mermaid:

Example: "What a beautiful day for me to swim and play!"

1. _____

2. _____

3. _____

4. _____

5. _____

Scenes for your Mermaid:

Example: (1) meet Splash as she begins her day under the sea (2) meet sharks Riptide and Undertoe (3) Splash goes to see her friends (4) Splash is chased by sharks (5) Splash gets away but gets stuck in cave (6) friends Coral, Crystal, and Kelp rescue Splash from the cave (7) Splash swims and plays with friends

1. _____

2. _____

3. _____

4. _____

5. _____

6. _____

7. _____

Mermaid - Script, Song, or Work of Art

In the space below, write a script, song, story, rap, or dance moves. On a separate piece of paper, you may design a costume, or draw a picture of your Mermaid.

Name:_____

_____

_____

_____

_____

_____

_____

_____

_____

_____

_____

_____

_____

_____

_____

_____

_____

_____

_____

_____

_____

Written by:_____

Meet the Knight

Create your own Knight

Answer the questions below to invent your own Knight.

❶What is your Knight's Name?
Example: My knight's name is Sir Pork of Chop.

_____

❷What kind of costume does your Knight wear?
Example: Sir Pork of Chop wears a suit of armor, a helmet, and carries a sheild.

_____

❸Where does your Knight live?
Example: Sir Pork of Chop lives just outside the Kingdom of Gladingham.

_____

❹What does your Knight do?
Example: Sir Pork of Chop guards the gates of the Kingdom.

_____

❺Does your Knight speak with an accent? If yes, what kind?
Example: Sir Pork of Chop speaks with an English accent.

_____

❻Who are your Knight's friends?
Example: Sir Pork of Chop's friends are his fellow knights.

_____

❼Does your Knight have any special abilities or powers?
Example: Sir Pork of Chop is very brave, and extremely skilled with the sword.

_____

Create your own Lines & Scenes

In the space below, create lines and scenes for your Knight.

Lines for your Knight:
Example: "Halt! Who goes there?"

1. _____

2. _____

3. _____

4. _____

5. _____

Scenes for your Knight:
Example: (1) meet young Sir Pork of Chop (2) outside the Kingdom, the dark knight approaches (3) the battle (4) Sir Pork of Chop is victorious (5) Sir Pork of Chop rides into the Kingdom to announce his victory to the King (6) feast in the great hall (7) the knighting of Sir Pork of Chop and celebration

1. _____

2. _____

3. _____

4. _____

5. _____

6. _____

7. _____

Knight - Script, Song, or Work of Art

In the space below, write a script, song, story, rap, or dance moves. On a separate piece of paper, you may design a costume or draw a picture of your Knight.

Name:_____

_____

_____

_____

_____

_____

_____

_____

_____

_____

_____

_____

_____

_____

_____

_____

_____

_____

_____

_____

_____

_____

Written by:_____

Meet the Ghost

www.playgroundtheatre.com

Create your own Ghost

Answer the questions below to invent your own Ghost.

❶What is your Ghost's Name?
Example: My ghost's name is Ghoulie.

_____

❷What kind of costume does your Ghost wear?
Example: Ghoulie wears a dark, ragged sheet that goes from over his head down to his toes.

_____

❸Where does your Ghost live?
Example: Ghoulie lives in a graveyard, deep in the hills of Translyvania.

_____

❹What does your Ghost do?
Example: Ghoulie likes to haunt old houses, and his favorite holiday is Halloween.

_____

❺Does your Ghost speak with an accent? If yes, what kind?
Example: Yes, Ghoulie speaks with a low moan.

_____

❻Who are your Ghost friends?
Example: Ghoulie is friends with Victor and Victoria Vampire.

_____

❼Does your Ghost have any special abilities or powers?
Example: Ghoulie can walk through walls, and turn into fog.

_____

 # Create your own Lines & Scenes

In the space below, create lines and scenes for your Ghost.

Lines for your Ghost:

Example: "Aaaaaahhh! Oooooohhhh! Oooooowwww!"

1. _____

2. _____

3. _____

4. _____

5. _____

Scenes for your Ghost:

Example: (1) meet Ghoulie (2) Ghoulie is invited to Victor Vampire's 500th birthday party (3) Ghoulie dresses up for the party (4) Ghoulie remembers to buy gift, and goes shopping (5) Ghoulie scares sales person, and runs out of store without gift (6) Ghoulie picks dead flowers (7) birthday party at the Vampires

1. _____

2. _____

3. _____

4. _____

5. _____

6. _____

7. _____

Ghost - Script, Song, or Work of Art

In the space below, write a script, song, story, rap, or dance moves.
On a separate piece of paper, you may design a costume or
draw a picture of your Ghost.

Name:_____

_____

_____

_____

_____

_____

_____

_____

_____

_____

_____

_____

_____

_____

_____

_____

_____

_____

_____

_____

_____

Written by:_____

Special thanks to illustrators and contributors: Andy Seery, Katrina van Pelt, Todd Bryan, and Dr. Barry Bennett

Meet the Authors and Founders of Play-Ground Theatre Company, Inc. Mia Sole & Jeff Haycock

Madcap. Energetic. Joyful. These are just a few of the adjectives that come instantly to mind when describing Mia Sole and Jeff Haycock, founders of Colorado's Play-Ground Theatre Company. They began writing, directing, and performing plays in the spirit of "Saturday Night Live" for kids, while providing acting workshops for all ages in 1989.

Over the years, Play-Ground Theatre's performances and programs for children have become increasingly popular. As they considered ways of meeting children's needs, they realized that they had been developing a curriculum to share – a program that captures the spirit of Play-Ground Theatre.

They now offer educators a drama program for preschool children ages 3-6, and a school age drama program for ages 7-12. These theatre programs include: self-study training manuals, marketing kit, CDs of songs and music, text books with complete lesson plans, scripts, costume accessories, handouts, and summer drama books.

Playground Theatre fosters not only a delight in the performing arts, but a powerful self-esteem that carries over into other activities and endeavors. Their motto is "Play-Ground Theatre: Changing the world one child at a time." Considering their successful work and play with children and adults, perhaps that motto should be revised to read: one *inner* child at a time.

For more information go to: www.playgroundtheatre.com
Or call our Colorado main office at: 303-258-0393

Play-Ground Theatre School Age Drama Program for Ages 7-12

You can host an innovative, energizing, motivating, and financially successful drama program that teachers, students, and parents love. Play-Ground School Age Drama Program for Ages 7-12 includes **everything** teachers need to easily make theatre a regular part of their classroom.

Training Manuals, Textbooks, Scripts, Costumes, Props, Music, Handouts, Summer Books and more! This program can be instructed during the school day or as an additional program after school.

Incorporate acting, dance, music, singing, performance, teamwork, and self-expression in a safe, positive environment. Students choose their own characters and perform plays with teachers for families and friends to enjoy. Preschool Drama Program for ages 3-6 is also available.

For more information go to: www.playgroundtheatre.com

Play-Ground Theatre Company, Inc.
Products & Services

Preschool Drama Program
For Ages 3-6

Complete Curriculum
$495
Staff Trainings Available
Call: 303.258.0393
More Information:
www.playgroundtheatre.com

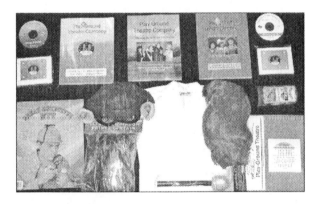

School Age Drama Program
For Ages 7-12

Complete Curriculum
$495
Staff Trainings Available
Call: 303.258.0393
More Information:
www.playgroundtheatre.com

The Best of Play-Ground
Theatre on DVD

- 3 Billy Goats Gruff
- Sleeping Beauty
- Rappin' Red Riding Hood
- Return of the Dodo Bird
- Pirates Treasure
- The Space Crusaders

Available on-line now! $14.99
www.playgroundtheatre.com

Wishing you great success
with Play-Ground Theatre Company's

Theatre Games for Elementary
School Children Ages 7-12